DOCTRINE & COVENANTS
STUDY GUIDE & ACTIVITY
BOOK FOR TEENS

ALIGNS WITH 2025 COME FOLLOW ME

TWO PAGES FOR EVERY COME FOLLOW ME LESSON FOR THE ENTIRE YEAR

THIS BOOK BELONGS TO:

_____

ABOUT THIS BOOK

This is an activity book and study guide for tweens & teens ages 11-18. There are two pages to complete that go along with the Come, Follow Me lesson each week.

MY GOALS FOR THIS YEAR

Write or draw your spiritual, physical, social, and intellectual goals for this year below.

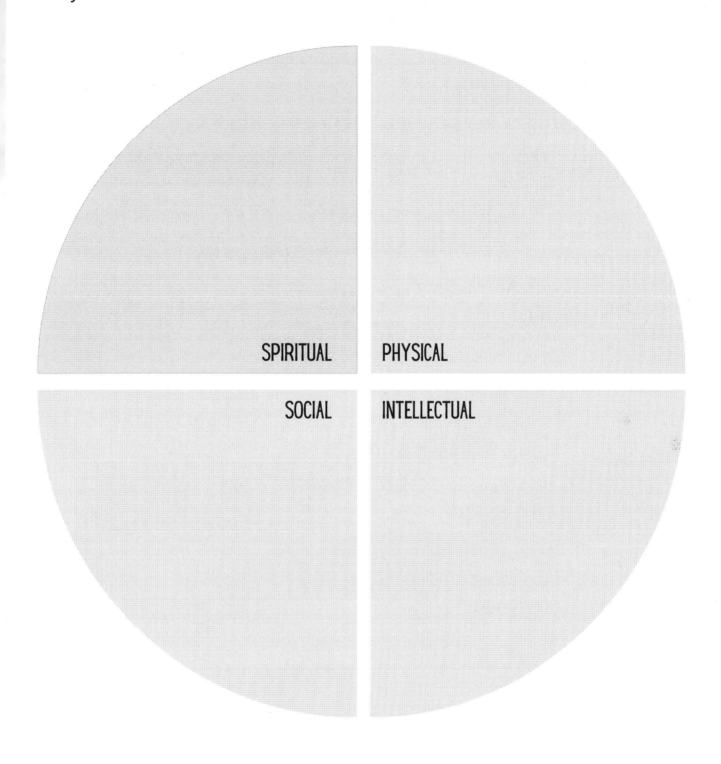

SPIRITUAL

PHYSICAL

SOCIAL

INTELLECTUAL

LESSON SCHEDULE

January
Dec 30-Jan 5	Restoration of the Gospel
Jan 6-12	D&C 1
Jan 13-19	JSH 1:1-26 & Voices of the Restoration: Joseph Smith's Family
Jan 20-26	D&C 2; JSH 1:27-65

February
Jan 27-Feb 2	D&C 3-5
Feb 3-9	D&C 6-9; Voices of the Restoration: Translation of the Book of Mormon
Feb 10-16	D&C 10-11
Feb 17-23	D&C 12-17; JSH 1:66-75; Voices of the Restoration: The Witnesses...

March
Feb 24-Mar 2	D&C 18
Mar 3-9	D&C 19
Mar 10-16	D&C 20-22
Mar 17-23	D&C 23-26; Voices of the Restoration: Emma Hale Smith
Mar 24-30	D&C 27-28

April
Mar 31-Apr 6	D&C 29
April 7-13	D&C 30-36; Voices of the Restoration: Early Converts
April 14-20	Easter
April 21-27	D&C 37-40; Voices of the Restoration: Gathering to Ohio

May
April 28-May 4	D&C 41-44
May 5-11	D&C 45
May 12-18	D&C 46-48
May 19-25	D&C 49-50

June
May 26-Jun 1	D&C 51-57
Jun 2-8	D&C 58-59
Jun 9-15	D&C 60-63
Jun 16-22	D&C 64-66
Jun 23-29	D&C 67-70

LESSON SCHEDULE

July
Jun 30-Jul 6   D&C 71-75

Jul 7-13   D&C 76; Voices of the Restoration: Testimonies of "the Vision"

Jul 14-20   D&C 77-80

Jul 21-27   D&C 81-83

August
Jul 28-Aug 3   D&C 84

Aug 4-10   D&C 85-87

Aug 11-17   D&C 88

Aug 18-24   D&C 89-92

Aug 25-31   D&C 93

September
Sept 1-7   D&C 94-97

Sept 8-14   D&C 98-101

Sept 15-21   D&C 102-105; Voices of the Restoration: Zion's Camp

Sept 22-28   D&C 106-108

October
Sept 29-Oct 5   D&C 109-110; Voices of the Restoration: ...and the Kirtland Temple

Oct 6-12   D&C 111-114

Oct 13-19   D&C 115-120

Oct 20-26   D&C 121-123; Voices of the Restoration: Liberty Jail

November
Oct 27-Nov 2   D&C 124; Voices of the Restoration: The Relief Society

Nov 3-9   D&C 125-128; Voices of the Restoration: Baptism for our Ancestors

Nov 10-16   D&C 129-132

Nov 17-23   D&C 133-134

Nov 24-30   D&C 135-136

December
Dec 1-7   D&C 137-138

Dec 8-14   Articles of Faith and Official Declarations 1 & 2

Dec 15-21   The Family: A Proclamation to the World

Dec 22-28   Christmas

EARLY CHURCH HISTORY TIMELINE

1805	JOSEPH SMITH BORN IN SHARON, VERMONT
1820	HEAVENLY FATHER & JESUS CHRIST APPEARED TO JOSEPH SMITH
1823	FIRST VISIT BY ANGEL MORONI TO JOSEPH SMITH
1827	JOSEPH SMITH RECEIVED THE GOLDEN PLATES
1829	THE TRANSLATION OF THE BOOK OF MORMON COMPLETED
1829	THE AARONIC AND MELCHIZEDEK PRIESTHOODS WERE RESTORED
1830	THE BOOK OF MORMON PUBLISHED
1830	THE CHURCH WAS ORGANIZED
1831	KIRTLAND, OHIO BECAME THE GATHERING PLACE FOR THE SAINTS
1831	INDEPENDENCE, MISSOURI CHOSEN BY LORD AS CITY OF ZION
1833	SAINTS FORCED TO LEAVE JACKSON COUNTY MISSOURI
1834	ZION'S CAMP GOES FROM OHIO TO MISSOURI
1835	QUORUM OF THE 12 APOSTLES & QUORUM OF THE SEVENTY ORGANIZED
1836	KIRTLAND TEMPLE DEDICATED
1836	PRIESTHOOD KEYS GIVEN TO JOSEPH SMITH AND OLIVER COWDERY IN THE TEMPLE
1838	JOSEPH SMITH AND OTHER CHURCH LEADERS MOVED TO FAR WEST, MISSOURI
1838	JOSEPH SMITH & FIVE OTHERS IMPRISONED IN LIBERTY JAIL
1839	THE SAINTS IN MISSOURI FORCED TO LEAVE THE STATE
1839	JOSEPH & COMPANIONS RELEASED FROM JAIL & GO TO ILLINOIS TO ESTABLISH NAUVOO
1840	ORDINANCE OF BAPTISM FOR THE DEAD BEGAN
1842	RELIEF SOCIETY ORGANIZED
1842	FULL ENDOWMENT ADMINISTERED TO CHURCH MEMBERS
1843	REVELATION ON ETERNAL MARRIAGE AND PLURAL WIVES RECORDED
1844	JOSEPH AND HYRUM SMITH ASSASSINATED
1844	THE QUORUM OF THE 12 APOSTLES SUSTAINED TO LEAD THE CHURCH
1846	MANY SAINTS START JOURNEY TO SALT LAKE CITY
1846	NAUVOO TEMPLE DEDICATED
1847	FIRST GROUP OF SAINTS ARRIVE IN SALT LAKE VALLEY

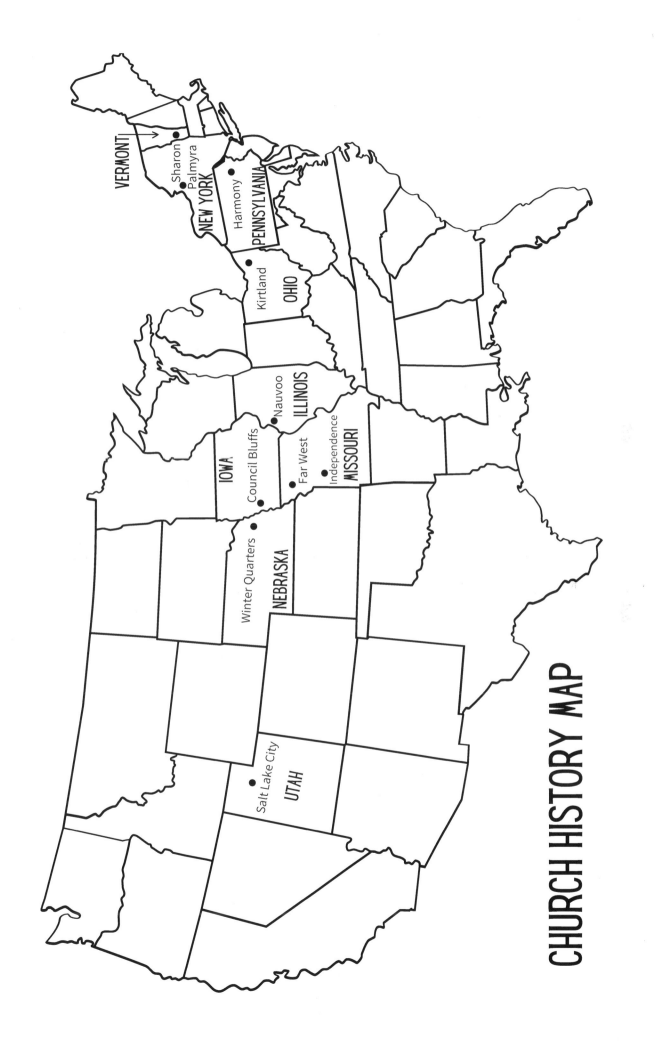

CHURCH HISTORY MAP

VERMONT

Sharon
Palmyra

NEW YORK

Harmony

PENNSYLVANIA

Kirtland

OHIO

Nauvoo

ILLINOIS

Council Bluffs

IOWA

Far West

Independence

MISSOURI

Winter Quarters

NEBRASKA

Salt Lake City

UTAH

DECEMBER 30 - JANUARY 5

CIRCLE THE DAYS YOU READ THIS WEEK: MON TUES WED THUR FRI SAT SUN

READ D&C 18:37-38; 107:23-24; 51:3; 70:14; 84:64-72; 110:11-16; 124:31, 36; 6TH ARTICLE OF FAITH

How is the Restored Church similar to Christ's Church in the New Testament?

_____

_____

_____

_____

_____

READ "THE RESTORATION OF THE FULNESS OF THE GOSPEL OF JESUS CHRIST: A BICENTENNIAL PROCLAMATION TO THE WORLD"

What do we learn about Jesus and the Restoration in these paragraphs?

_____

_____

_____

_____

_____

READ "ARE YOU SLEEPING THROUGH THE RESTORATION?" BY ELDER UCHTDORF FROM THE ENISGN OR LIAHONA, MAY 2014

What three things are mentioned in this talk that may cause us to sleep through the Restoration?

_____

_____

_____

Write your study plan for reading the Doctrine & Covenants this year. When and how will you study? Do you have specific things you are looking for in your study?

_____

_____

_____

_____

RESTORATION OF THE GOSPEL

Joseph Smith had questions. We are blessed today because Joseph asked questions! What questions do you have? Joseph learned in James 1:5 what to do when you have a question...read the scriptures & ask God! Below, write questions you have & then go to the scriptures and read & pray like Joseph did to get answers. These answers may take time, so come back to this page and write answers as you receive them.

WHICH CHURCH SHOULD I JOIN?

QUESTIONS I HAVE:

_____
_____
_____
_____
_____
_____
_____
_____
_____

SCRIPTURES I READ FOR ANSWERS & INSPIRATION I RECEIVED THROUGH PRAYER:

_____
_____
_____
_____
_____
_____
_____
_____
_____

JANUARY 6-12

Read D&C 1:1-10. Can you think of warning signs you have seen? Road signs let us know about curves ahead so we know to slow down. After mopping a floor, janitors often put out signs to let us know the floor is slippery. The prophets also give us warnings the Lord wants us to know. On the signs below, write some warnings the prophets & apostles have given to us in recent general conference addresses.

THE LORD WARNS US OF SPIRITUAL DANGERS THROUGH HIS PROPHETS

D&C 1

READ THE INTRODUCTION TO THE DOCTRINE AND COVENANTS
What is the purpose of the revelations in the Doctrine & Covenants?

_____

_____

_____

_____

_____

READ THE TESTIMONY OF THE 12 APOSTLES IN THE INTRODUCTION TO THE D&C
What stands out to you in the testimony of the apostles?

_____

_____

_____

_____

_____

READ D&C 1:11-20
How can we prepare for the coming of the Lord?

_____

_____

_____

_____

READ D&C 1:31-39
What does it mean that the Church is "true and living"?

_____

_____

_____

_____

JANUARY 13-19

CIRCLE THE DAYS YOU READ THIS WEEK: MON TUES WED THUR FRI SAT SUN

Joseph Smith was born December 23, 1805, in Vermont to Joseph Smith, Sr. and Lucy Mack Smith. They were good parents who loved God. Joseph had five brothers & three sisters. Draw faces on Joseph's family below and color.

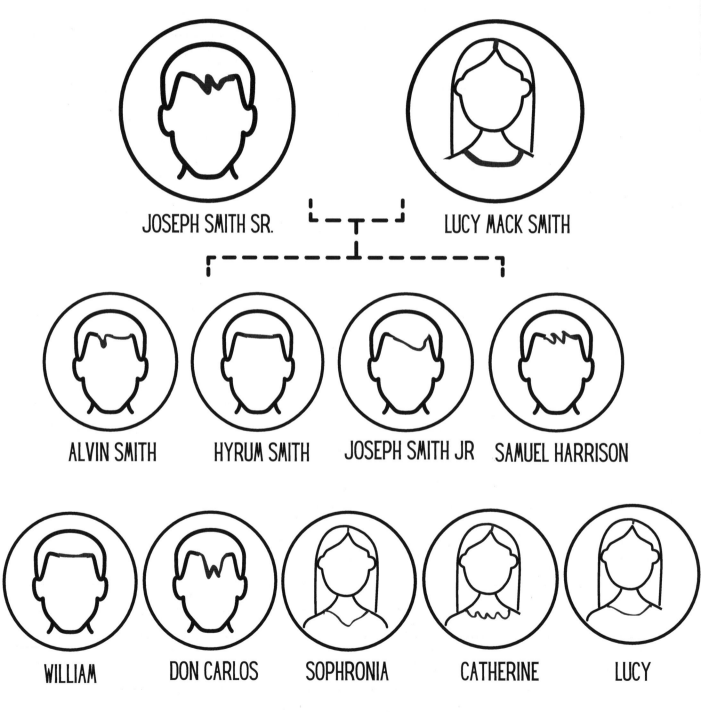

JOSEPH SMITH SR.   LUCY MACK SMITH

ALVIN SMITH   HYRUM SMITH   JOSEPH SMITH JR   SAMUEL HARRISON

WILLIAM   DON CARLOS   SOPHRONIA   CATHERINE   LUCY

JOSEPH SMITH WAS PREPARED TO BE A PROPHET

JSH 1:1-26 &
VOICES OF THE RESTORATON: JOSEPH SMITH'S FAMILY

READ JOSEPH SMITH HISTORY 1:1-14

What can we learn from Joseph about how to prepare to receive personal revelation?

_____

_____

_____

_____

_____

READ JOSEPH SMITH HISTORY 1:15–26

What truths do you know because of the First Vision?

_____

_____

_____

_____

_____

READ "NOURISHING AND BEARING YOUR TESTIMONY" BY ELDER STEVENSON FROM THE ENSIGN OR LIAHONA, NOV. 2022

How can you remain true to your testimony when others oppose your beliefs?

_____

_____

_____

_____

_____

READ VOICES OF THE RESTORATION: JOSEPH SMITH'S FAMILY

What do you learn about the character of Joseph's mother and father?

_____

_____

_____

_____

_____

JANUARY 20-26

READ JOSEPH SMITH HISTORY 1:27-33

Do you ever feel like Joseph did? What work does God have for you to do?

_____

_____

_____

_____

_____

_____

READ JOSEPH SMITH HISTORY 1:34-47

Why were the prophecies (from the Bible) Moroni quoted to Joseph important?

_____

_____

_____

_____

_____

_____

READ JOSEPH SMITH HISTORY 1:48-60

What events have happened in your life to prepare you to serve God and others?

_____

_____

_____

_____

_____

READ JOSEPH SMITH HISTORY 1:61-65

Why did Martin Harris take a translation of the plates to Professor Anthon?

_____

_____

_____

_____

_____

_____

D&C 2; JSH 1:27-65

In D&C 2, we learn about the mission of Elijah to turn the hearts of the children to their fathers. One way we can do this is through learning about our ancestors. Ask your family to share some stories with you about your ancestors. Fill out the family tree below and write your name and the names of your family. Spend some time on familysearch.org and learn about one of your ancestors.

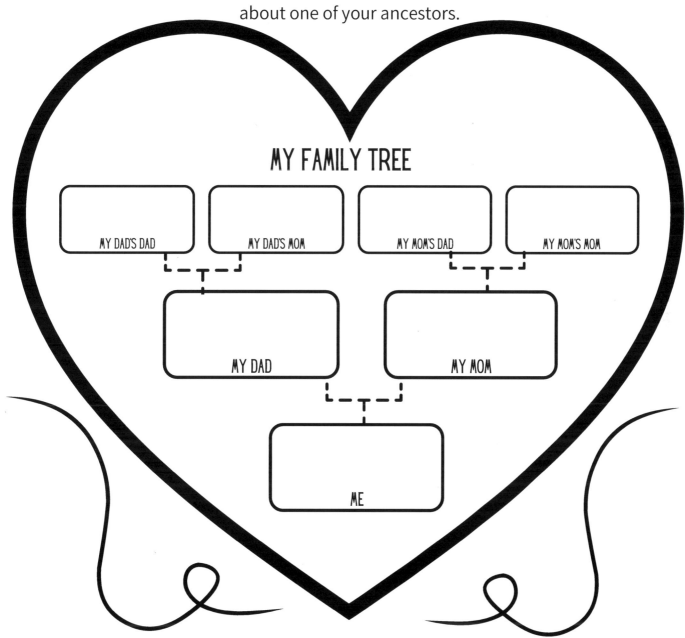

MY FAMILY TREE

| MY DAD'S DAD | MY DAD'S MOM | MY MOM'S DAD | MY MOM'S MOM |

| MY DAD | MY MOM |

ME

I CAN FEEL JOY BY LEARNING ABOUT MY ANCESTORS

JANUARY 27-FEBRUARY 2

CIRCLE THE DAYS YOU READ THIS WEEK: MON TUES WED THUR FRI SAT SUN

READ D&C 3:1-10

What are the consequences of fearing man more than God?

_____

_____

_____

_____

_____

_____

READ D&C 3:11-20

How will the Lord's work go forth?

_____

_____

_____

_____

_____

_____

READ D&C 4

What qualities is the Lord looking for in His servants?

_____

_____

_____

_____

_____

_____

READ D&C 5:1-19

How can we be witnesses of the Book of Mormon?

_____

_____

_____

_____

D&C 3-5

Joseph gave his friend Martin Harris 116 pages of the translation of the Book of Mormon to show to his wife. The pages were lost and Joseph and Martin were chastised by the Lord. What do you learn from this account about trusting God and not giving into peer pressure? Complete the word search below.

```
W  O  U  V  F  A  I  V  C  X  G  W  F  B  O
B  P  Y  O  L  F  C  J  X  Z  P  Y  X  F  V
Z  Q  N  A  P  O  D  J  E  G  A  D  C  N  R
I  V  D  E  T  B  T  U  J  A  G  V  Z  P  R
J  G  V  V  G  N  M  F  T  N  E  X  Z  R  K
P  R  I  I  N  D  E  S  I  T  S  A  H  C  C
L  W  K  G  C  I  U  P  L  A  U  T  P  L  W
S  H  X  R  D  R  W  H  E  V  R  U  B  G  O
H  Y  J  O  T  W  M  E  H  R  I  O  U  D  Q
A  F  J  F  L  S  U  K  M  I  W  O  Z  C  C
U  Q  P  M  Z  T  O  Q  A  C  Q  X  D  J  M
R  V  X  M  O  X  C  L  L  H  W  R  J  H  V
N  Q  E  G  F  Y  O  D  T  I  V  O  H  A  K
Z  F  D  A  M  R  H  P  E  S  O  J  U  I  N
I  N  D  Y  D  E  M  K  Z  M  A  R  T  I  N
```

JOSEPH	MARTIN	PAGES
LOST	LORD	CHASTISED
REPENT	TRUST	FORGIVE

I CAN CHOOSE THE RIGHT EVEN WHEN OTHERS TRY TO GET ME TO CHOOSE WRONG

FEBRUARY 3-9

CIRCLE THE DAYS YOU READ THIS WEEK: MON TUES WED THUR FRI SAT SUN

READ D&C 6:1-19

What do we learn about receiving personal revelation in these verses?

_____

_____

_____

_____

_____

READ D&C 6:20-37

How does God feel about our righteous desires?

_____

_____

_____

_____

_____

READ D&C 9

Why did the Lord take away Oliver's privilege to translate?

_____

_____

_____

_____

_____

READ VOICES OF THE RESTORATION: TRANSLATION OF THE BOOK OF MORMON

What stood out to you in Emma's account of translating the Book of Mormon?

_____

_____

_____

_____

_____

D&C 6-9; VOICES OF THE RESTORATION: TRANSLATION OF THE BOOK OF MORMON

Complete the cross-word puzzle below with words that relate to this week's reading.

DOWN

1-IN SECTION 6, THE LORD SAYS "FEAR NOT, LITTLE _____"

2-IN SECTION 6, THE LORD TELLS OLIVER HE HAS GIVEN HIM A _____OF THE TRUTH OF THE PLATES.

ACROSS

3-THE FIRST NAME OF JOSEPH SMITH'S SCRIBE.

4-THE HOLY GHOST CAN COMMUNICATE WITH YOU THROUGH YOUR MIND & _____

I CAN LOOK TO JESUS IN EVERY THOUGHT

FEBRUARY 10-16

CIRCLE THE DAYS YOU READ THIS WEEK: MON TUES WED THUR FRI SAT SUN

READ D&C 10:1-15

Why should we "pray always"? How do we "pray always"?

_____

_____

_____

_____

_____

READ D&C 10:16-33

What do we learn about Satan and his methods for attacking truth?

_____

_____

_____

_____

_____

READ D&C 10:34-51

What do we learn about the Lord's wisdom in these verses, regarding the lost 116 pages?

_____

_____

_____

_____

_____

READ D&C 11:1-14

What do you learn about personal revelation in these verses?

_____

_____

_____

_____

_____

In D&C 11:12-13, we are told the Holy Ghost "enlightens" our minds and fills our souls "with joy". Color the verse below.

"...Spirit ...leadeth ...to do good... shall enlighten your mind ...fill your soul with joy"

FEBRUARY 17-23

In D&C 13:1, we read about John the Baptist restoring the Aaronic priesthood. Fill in the missing words from this scripture passage below. What blessings have you received from priesthood ordinances?

"UPON YOU MY FELLOW _____, IN THE NAME OF _____I CONFER THE PRIESTHOOD OF _____, WHICH HOLDS THE _____OF THE MINISTERING OF _____, AND OF THE GOSPEL OF _____, AND OF _____BY IMMERSION FOR THE _____OF SINS; AND THIS SHALL NEVER BE TAKEN AGAIN FROM THE _____, UNTIL THE SONS OF _____DO OFFER AGAIN AN _____UNTO THE _____IN RIGHTEOUSNESS."

D&C 13:1

D&C 12-17; JSH 1:66-75; VOICES OF THE RESTORATION: THE WITNESSES OF THE BOOK OF MORMON

READ D&C 14

How can you stand as a witness?

_____

_____

_____

_____

_____

_____

READ D&C 15-16

What is the "thing which will be of the most worth"?

_____

_____

_____

_____

_____

_____

READ D&C 17

What were the three witnesses told to do?

_____

_____

_____

_____

_____

READ VOICES OF THE RESTORATION: WITNESSES OF THE BOOK OF MORMON

What stood out to you from the words of the witnesses of the Book of Mormon?

_____

_____

_____

_____

_____

FEBRUARY 24-MARCH 2

CIRCLE THE DAYS YOU READ THIS WEEK: MON TUES WED THUR FRI SAT SUN

READ D&C 18:1-9

How do you build your foundation upon the Savior's "rock"?

_____

_____

_____

_____

_____

READ ALMA 36:18-21 & D&C 18:11-16

What is repentance? What do you learn in these verses?

_____

_____

_____

_____

_____

READ D&C 18:20-29

Why should we not "contend"?

_____

_____

_____

_____

_____

READ D&C 18:30-39

What does the voice of the Lord sound like to you?

_____

_____

_____

_____

_____

D&C 18

In D&C 18:13–16, we read that sharing the gospel with others and bringing them to Christ brings us joy. Color the picture of the missionaries below. Write ways you can or have shared the gospel in the ovals below.

SHARING THE GOSPEL BRINGS ME JOY

MARCH 3-9

CIRCLE THE DAYS YOU READ THIS WEEK: MON TUES WED THUR FRI SAT SUN

READ D&C 19:1-12

What do we learn about God's eternal nature in these verses?

_____

_____

_____

_____

_____

_____

READ D&C 19:13-20

What do you learn about the Atonement?

_____

_____

_____

_____

_____

_____

READ D&C 19:21-30

What does it mean to "walk in the meekness" of the Spirit?

_____

_____

_____

_____

_____

READ "FINDING PERSONAL PEACE," BY HENRY B. EYRING, ENSIGN OR LIAHONA, MAY 2023

What stood out to you in this talk by Pres. Eyring?

_____

_____

_____

_____

_____

_____

D&C 19

In D&C 19:26–41, we read about the sacrifice Martin Harris made in having to sell a large portion of his farm to pay the printer for the copies of the Book of Mormon. What sacrifices does the Lord ask you to make? The Lord tells us that His blessings are greater than the treasures of the earth. Color the treasure box and list some of the blessings God gives you in the coins.

GOD'S BLESSINGS ARE GREATER THAN THE TREASURES OF THE EARTH

MARCH 10-16

READ D&C 20:1-20

What do we learn about the organization of the Savior's restored Church?

_____

_____

_____

_____

_____

READ D&C 20:21-40

How do ordinances help us feel connected to the Savior?

_____

_____

_____

_____

_____

READ D&C 20:61-84

What do you learn from the sacrament prayers?

_____

_____

_____

_____

_____

READ D&C 21

What has the Lord asked us to do through our current prophet?

_____

_____

_____

_____

_____

D&C 20-22

In D&C 20:37, 41, 71–74, we learn about being baptized and receiving the gift of the Holy Ghost. Complete the word search below.

BAPTISMAL COVENANTS

I PROMISE TO:
- TAKE CHRIST'S NAME UPON ME
- SERVE THE LORD & OTHERS
- OBEY COMMANDMENTS

HEAVENLY FATHER PROMISES TO:
- FORGIVE ME WHEN I MAKE MISTAKES
- GIVE ME THE COMPANIONSHIP OF THE HOLY GHOST
- MAKE IT POSSIBLE FOR ME TO LIVE WITH HIM AGAIN

```
J  I  A  L  W  L  V  Z  T  U  V  K  O  J  Q  T  T  O  C  C
G  C  J  H  N  X  V  I  I  W  O  P  Y  E  B  O  T  Z  Q  N
Z  K  L  S  F  X  H  G  C  C  L  V  R  K  R  T  E  T  N  A
V  V  R  X  E  Q  K  Y  H  X  P  T  M  E  B  J  K  P  L  K
L  B  F  O  Q  K  L  J  P  D  J  X  R  L  G  K  T  Q  K  O
K  W  S  Y  U  F  F  S  R  P  V  E  I  A  F  A  I  U  X  D
D  X  F  I  W  H  E  O  D  P  P  K  S  M  Y  D  E  Y  E  I
P  G  B  R  R  M  L  D  K  E  W  D  T  S  M  Z  Q  W  T  D
R  F  O  R  G  I  V  E  N  E  S  S  N  I  S  K  J  A  S  F
O  O  A  Z  A  R  O  T  A  S  T  E  A  T  W  Q  I  I  R  I
M  K  L  K  Z  T  A  N  D  N  E  I  N  P  G  F  U  W  G  T
I  W  W  L  T  N  O  D  E  R  V  R  E  A  T  C  B  Q  G  R
S  S  B  D  C  P  E  M  C  V  W  T  V  B  D  H  D  Z  E  M
E  O  O  E  A  U  D  F  F  P  L  Z  O  E  R  G  L  P  O  F
M  Y  X  V  I  N  T  B  N  O  K  A  C  I  X  S  W  R  X  M
W  Y  B  V  A  H  C  T  S  Q  I  G  F  J  J  Y  Z  S  U  Z
S  G  L  M  V  I  I  Y  S  P  U  G  U  A  H  X  P  A  W  R
U  I  M  X  K  Z  A  K  N  B  A  K  Z  X  A  Y  I  H  U  Z
H  O  C  V  F  H  Z  U  L  N  L  A  S  O  N  A  E  J  K  O
C  Z  Y  T  C  O  S  M  G  U  G  M  P  L  Z  W  H  M  S  H
```

BAPTISMAL	COVENANTS	PROMISE
SERVE	LORD	OBEY
COMMANDMENTS	REPENTANCE	FORGIVENESS

In D&C 25, the Lord gives Emma counsel on what he would like her to do. Color the picture of Emma below and some of the things she was asked to do by the Lord.

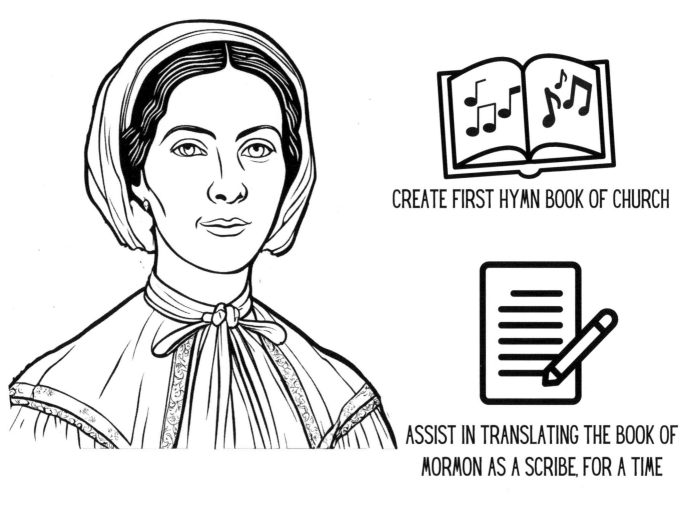

CREATE FIRST HYMN BOOK OF CHURCH

ASSIST IN TRANSLATING THE BOOK OF MORMON AS A SCRIBE, FOR A TIME

COMFORT THE PROPHET JOSEPH IN HIS AFFLICTIONS

EMMA HALE SMITH WAS AN ELECT LADY

D&C 23-26;
VOICES OF THE RESTORATION: EMMA HALE SMITH

READ D&C 23

What does it mean to "take up your cross"?

_____
_____
_____
_____
_____
_____

READ D&C 24:1-9

How can the Savior help you in your afflictions?

_____
_____
_____
_____
_____
_____

READ D&C 24:10-19

How does the Lord bless and protect His missionaries?

_____
_____
_____
_____
_____
_____

READ VOICES OF THE RESTORATION: EMMA HALE SMITH

What stands out to you about Emma?

_____
_____
_____
_____
_____

MARCH 24-30

In D&C 27, we learn about how the armor of God protects us. On the armor below, fill in the missing word for each piece of armor that describes how it spiritually protects us. Use D&C 27 to help you find the missing words.

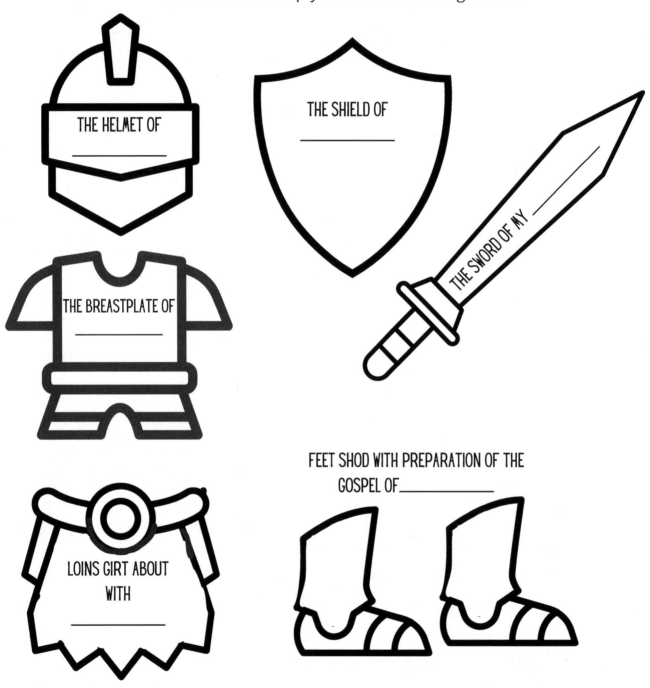

THE HELMET OF
_____

THE SHIELD OF
_____

THE BREASTPLATE OF
_____

THE SWORD OF MY _____

LOINS GIRT ABOUT WITH
_____

FEET SHOD WITH PREPARATION OF THE GOSPEL OF_____

THE ARMOR OF GOD PROTECTS ME

D&C 27-28

READ D&C 27:1-4; LUKE 22:19-20; 3 NEPHI 18:1-11

How do you think the Savior wants us to approach the sacrament?

_____
_____
_____
_____
_____
_____

READ D&C 27:5-14

Learn about the prophets listed in these verses. What keys did these prophets hold?

_____
_____
_____
_____
_____
_____

READ D&C 28:8-16

Why was a mission to the Lamanites important?

_____
_____
_____
_____
_____
_____

READ JOHN 14:26; MORONI 8:26; 10:4-5

How does the Holy Ghost Guide you? Can you think of a specific experience?

_____
_____
_____
_____
_____

MARCH 31-APRIL 6

CIRCLE THE DAYS YOU READ THIS WEEK: MON TUES WED THUR FRI SAT SUN

READ D&C 29:1-11

Who will be gathered? Why are we gathered to Christ?

_____

_____

_____

_____

_____

READ "HOPE OF ISRAEL" BY PRES. & SISTER NELSON, (WORLDWIDE YTH. DEVOTIONAL, JUNE 2018), GOSPEL LIBRARY

What did impressions do you have after reading the talk?

_____

_____

_____

_____

_____

_____

READ D&C 29:12-20

What signs will precede the Second Coming?

_____

_____

_____

_____

_____

READ D&C 29:21-30

Do you feel prepared for the Second Coming? Why or why not?

_____

_____

_____

_____

_____

D&C 29

In D&C 29:11, Jesus tells us He will come again. Fill in the missing words for this scripture verse below and see if you can memorize it!

"FOR I WILL REVEAL MYSELF FROM
_____WITH _____ AND GREAT
_____, WITH ALL THE HOSTS THEREOF,
AND DWELL IN _____WITH MEN ON
EARTH A _____ YEARS, AND THE
_____ SHALL NOT STAND."
-D&C 29:11

WICKED   RIGHTEOUSNESS   POWER   HEAVEN   THOUSAND   GLORY

WRITE WAYS YOU CAN FOLLOW IN CHRIST'S
FOOTSTEPS & PREPARE FOR HIM COMING AGAIN:

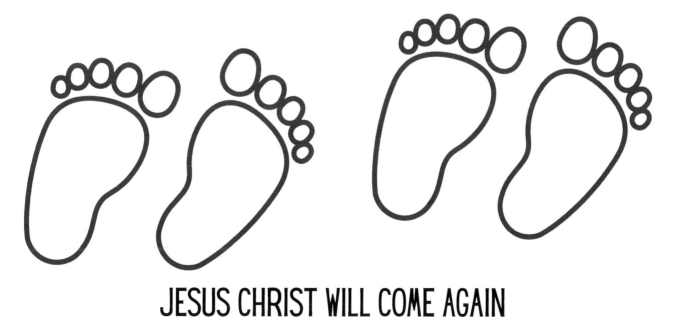

JESUS CHRIST WILL COME AGAIN

APRIL 7-13

In D&C 33:8-10, the Lord gives us advice on sharing the gospel with others. Crack the code below to find out what that message is. Discuss with your family what you think the message means.

CRACK THE CODE

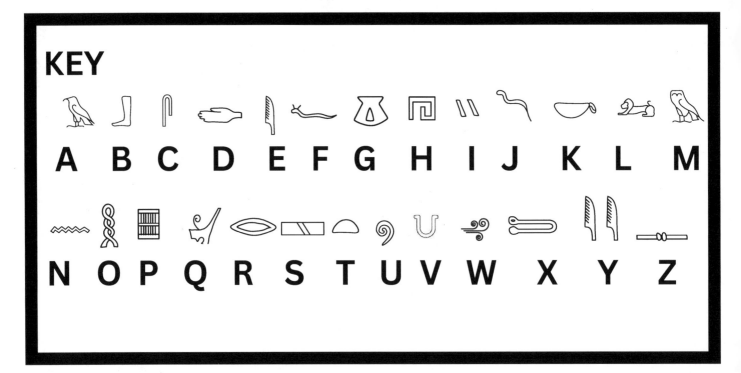

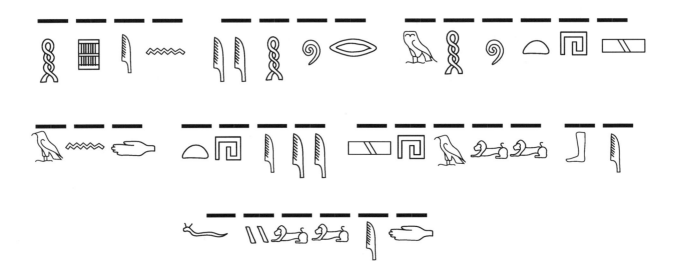

D&C 30-36;
VOICES OF THE RESTORATION: EARLY CONVERTS

READ D&C 30

What are some "things of the earth" that can distract us from the Savior?

_____

_____

_____

_____

_____

_____

READ D&C 31-32

How can the Lord help us with our family relationships?

_____

_____

_____

_____

_____

_____

READ D&C 34

How does remembering you are a son or daughter of God help you in this life?

_____

_____

_____

_____

_____

_____

READ D&C 36 & VOICES OF THE RESTORATION: EARLY CONVERTS

What do you learn from these early converts?

_____

_____

_____

_____

_____

CIRCLE THE DAYS YOU READ THIS WEEK: MON TUES WED THUR FRI SAT SUN

Put the events of Holy Week in order below, by numbering the first event with a "1" and the second event with a "2" and so forth. Ask your family for assistance, if needed. You can also reference Matthew chapters 21-28.

#___

RESURRECTED JESUS APPEARS TO MARY MAGDALENE

#___

JESUS SUFFERS FOR OUR SINS IN GARDEN OF GETHSEMANE

#___

JESUS TEACHES THE PEOPLE PARABLES

#___

JESUS IS RESURRECTED & HIS BODY PLACED IN A TOMB

#___

JESUS TRIUMPHAL ENTRY INTO JERUSALEM ON A DONKEY & PEOPLE WAVING PALM BRANCHES

#___

JESUS INTRODUCED THE ORDINANCE OF THE SACRAMENT TO HIS APOSTLES AT THE LAST SUPPER

EASTER

READ "THE LIVING CHRIST: THE TESTIMONY OF THE APOSTLES"
Who is Jesus Christ to you?

_____
_____
_____
_____
_____

READ DOCTRINE AND COVENANTS 76:11-14, 20-24; 110:1-10
How do others' testimonies of the Savior strengthen yours?

_____
_____
_____
_____
_____

READ ISAIAH 53:3-5; HEBREWS 2:17-18; MOSIAH 3:7; ALMA 7:11-13; 36:3; ETHER 12:27
How can the Savior help you?

_____
_____
_____
_____
_____

READ LUKE 22:39-44; 1 JOHN 1:7; 2 NEPHI 2:6-9; MOSIAH 3:5-13, 17-18; MORONI 10:32-33
What is the Atonement of Jesus Christ? What does it mean to you?

_____
_____
_____
_____

APRIL 21-27

In D&C 37-38, we read about members of the Church having to make sacrifices to gather in Ohio. They didn't have cars and planes back then, so it was a big effort to move that far away. Why do you think the Lord likes to gather His people? Write **10 items** below that you would take with you if you were one of the early Saints moving to Ohio.

10 ITEMS I WOULD BRING WITH ME IF I WERE AN EARLY SAINT MOVING FROM NEW YORK TO OHIO:

1- _____

2- _____

3- _____

4- _____

5- _____

6- _____

7- _____

8- _____

9- _____

10- _____

THE LORD GATHERS US TO BLESS US

D&C 37-40;
VOICES OF THE RESTORATION: GATHERING TO OHIO

READ D&C 27; VOICES OF THE RESTORATION: GATHERING TO OHIO

What do you learn about faith from Phebe Carter?

_____

_____

_____

_____

_____

_____

READ D&C 38:1-22

How does following God's laws make you free? See verse 22.

_____

_____

_____

_____

_____

_____

READ D&C 38:23-42

If we are prepared, why should we not fear life's challenges?

_____

_____

_____

_____

_____

_____

READ D&C 40

Do the "cares of the world" and "fear of persecution" ever stop you from living the gospel? How so?

_____

_____

_____

_____

APRIL 28-MAY 4

CIRCLE THE DAYS YOU READ THIS WEEK: MON TUES WED THUR FRI SAT SUN

READ D&C 41
What does it mean to be a disciple of Christ?

_____

_____

_____

_____

_____

READ D&C 42:1-29
Why does God give us laws and commandments?

_____

_____

_____

_____

_____

READ D&C 42:61-93
What do you learn about revelation in these verses?

_____

_____

_____

_____

_____

READ D&C 43:1-20
What do you learn about prophets in these verses?

_____

_____

_____

_____

D&C 41-44

In D&C 42:30-42, we learn that we are to share with the poor. One way you help serve those in need is to fast once per month for two meals and give the money you would have spent on those two meals as a fast offering. The Church then uses that money to help those in need. Draw two meals on the plates below and how much each of those meals would cost.

HOW MUCH WOULD THESE TWO MEALS COST? _____

FAST OFFERINGS GIVE FOOD, CLOTHING, AND NECESSITIES TO THOSE WHO ARE POOR AND NEEDY.

CHRIST WANTS ME TO HELP THE POOR

MAY 5-11

CIRCLE THE DAYS YOU READ THIS WEEK: MON TUES WED THUR FRI SAT SUN

READ D&C 45:1-5; MORONI 7:27-28; D&C 29:5; 62:1

What is an advocate? How is Jesus our advocate with God?

_____

_____

_____

_____

_____

_____

READ D&C 45:24-40

What are your "holy places"? Can you make wherever you are more holy?

_____

_____

_____

_____

_____

_____

READ D&C 45:41-60

What are some of the signs and wonders of Christ's Second Coming?

_____

_____

_____

_____

_____

READ "IF YE HAD KNOWN ME," BY DAVID A. BEDNAR, ENSIGN OR LIAHONA, NOV. 2016

What are you going to apply to your life from this talk by Elder Bednar?

_____

_____

_____

_____

_____

D&C 45

Read the following scripture verses in D&C 45 that teach about the Second Coming. Match each scripture passage to the corresponding image.

D&C 45:44-45

D&C 45:51-52

D&C 45:55

D&C 45:58-59

D&C 45:66-71

JESUS WILL COME AGAIN

MAY 12-18

In D&C 46:13-26, we learn that the Lord has given each of us spiritual gifts to bless the lives of those around us. In the boxes below, color gifts you think you have. In the blank gift boxes, write a gift you have that is not listed. If you are unsure, talk with your family about gifts they think you have.

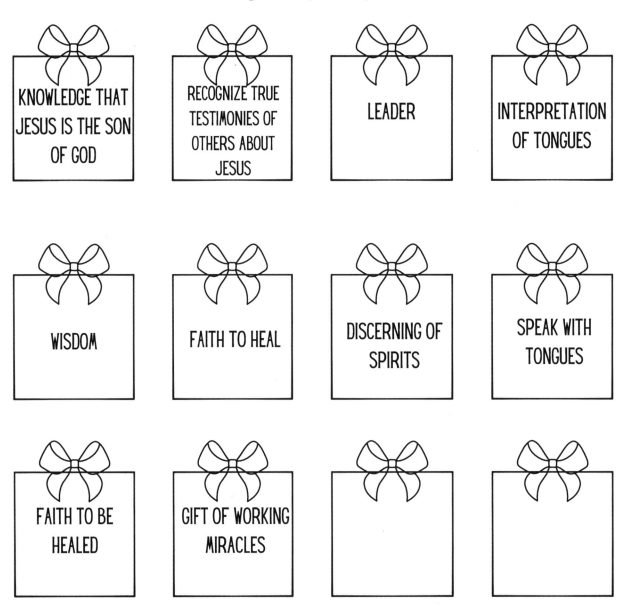

KNOWLEDGE THAT JESUS IS THE SON OF GOD

RECOGNIZE TRUE TESTIMONIES OF OTHERS ABOUT JESUS

LEADER

INTERPRETATION OF TONGUES

WISDOM

FAITH TO HEAL

DISCERNING OF SPIRITS

SPEAK WITH TONGUES

FAITH TO BE HEALED

GIFT OF WORKING MIRACLES

I HAVE BEEN GIVEN SPIRITUAL GIFTS TO BLESS OTHERS

D&C 46-48

READ D&C 46:1-7; 2 NEPHI 26:24-28; 3 NEPHI 18:22-23

What do you do to make people feel welcome at church?

_____

_____

_____

_____

_____

READ D&C 47

Why is keeping a history important to the Lord? Are you keeping a history of your life?

_____

_____

_____

_____

_____

READ "O REMEMBER, REMEMBER," BY HENRY B. EYRING, ENSIGN OR LIAHONA, NOV. 2007

What are you going to apply from this talk to your own life?

_____

_____

_____

_____

_____

READ D&C 48

What were the Saints commanded to do in this chapter?

_____

_____

_____

_____

_____

MAY 19-25

In D&C 49:12-14, we read ways we can follow Jesus Christ. Find some of these ways as you complete the crossword puzzle below.

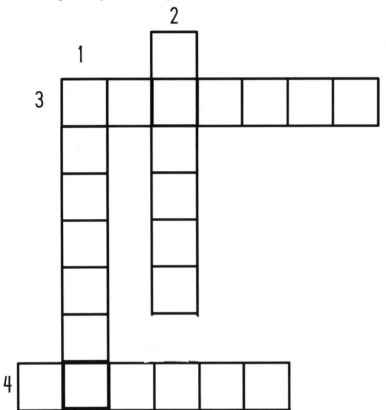

DOWN

1-THIS IS ANOTHER WORD FOR FAITH IN JESUS

2-THIS MEMBER OF THE GODHEAD HELPS GUIDE US THROUGH PROMPTINGS

ACROSS

3-THIS IS THE FIRST ORDINANCE OF THE GOSPEL WE MUST DO TO RECEIVE SALVATION

4-WE SHOULD DO THIS AFTER WE MAKE A MISTAKE

I CAN FOLLOW JESUS

D&C 49-50

READ D&C 49:1-14

How do your actions show that you are a follower of Jesus Christ?

_____

_____

_____

_____

_____

READ D&C 50:1-10

What "false spirits" and "hypocrites" do you see around you?

_____

_____

_____

_____

_____

READ D&C 50:11-22

How can we discern if something is from God?

_____

_____

_____

_____

_____

READ D&C 50:23-32

How can we receive God's light and chase away darkness in our lives?

_____

_____

_____

_____

_____

MAY 26-JUNE 1

READ D&C 51

How can you be a wise steward with all the Lord has entrusted you with?

_____

_____

_____

_____

_____

READ D&C 52:1-21

How can you know when you are being deceived?

_____

_____

_____

_____

_____

READ D&C 55 & 56

What counsel does the Lord give to the rich and poor?

_____

_____

_____

_____

_____

READ D&C 57

What is the significance of Independence, Missouri?

_____

_____

_____

_____

_____

D&C 51-57

In D&C 54, we learn about the frustration and disappointment the Saints from Colesville, New York experienced when they moved to Ohio and expected to settle on Leman Copley's land. Leman broke his promise and the Saints had to find somewhere else to settle. Complete word search below with words related to the reading.

```
X  O  D  B  A  X  C  Y  I  O  W  M  A  K  X  E  R  E  D  Q
F  P  I  C  A  R  I  G  V  K  H  M  Q  D  E  K  O  R  B  H
W  R  S  M  W  H  I  D  S  N  A  I  Z  G  B  Z  H  F  Q  O
N  M  A  O  G  A  N  Y  J  X  E  K  O  I  J  O  O  J  T  V
D  Z  P  D  U  J  I  M  P  P  Z  E  F  L  E  P  V  R  Y  P
R  X  P  B  R  R  L  S  J  W  S  U  L  F  S  A  M  N  E  J
D  E  O  R  J  A  C  K  X  B  P  T  S  G  Z  Y  E  X  L  C
T  L  I  I  O  P  W  I  P  N  E  W  N  Q  V  I  J  V  P  K
V  T  N  P  Q  M  G  M  Q  J  Y  O  Y  I  J  S  N  O  O  K
Z  A  T  O  H  E  I  K  H  W  D  M  G  G  A  G  W  B  C  M
M  E  E  G  G  B  Z  S  K  K  N  Q  J  E  N  S  I  N  I  E
Q  R  D  G  D  Q  N  X  E  Z  W  P  B  K  O  P  N  V  Z  P
Z  B  G  O  N  Q  T  F  K  P  F  X  W  B  J  K  Q  C  K  L
B  R  N  T  A  B  L  I  R  D  I  I  V  T  E  E  D  O  T  K
R  Q  Y  N  L  E  R  T  X  I  D  S  R  J  B  N  K  A  N  R
W  R  A  G  D  L  H  G  L  J  Z  Q  K  U  U  P  I  C  Z  W
W  A  J  B  W  O  K  M  W  H  A  J  S  P  F  X  J  M  R  C
I  L  R  Z  U  W  Q  I  V  G  I  C  C  X  H  U  U  A  K  Q
X  E  L  L  I  V  S  E  L  O  C  C  X  O  N  J  X  D  B  B
P  P  K  D  Q  P  S  M  K  W  A  Z  E  S  E  H  E  F  Y  V
```

COLESVILLE	SAINTS	MOVE
OHIO	COPLEY	LAND
BROKE	PROMISE	DISAPPOINTED

I CAN TURN TO THE LORD WHEN HURT BY OTHERS

JUNE 2-8

In D&C 58:26-28, we learn that we have the power to make our own choices. Write the consequences of each of the choices listed below.

CHOICE

READING SCRIPTURES

CHEATING ON A TEST

PRAYING

STAYING UP WAY PAST BEDTIME

CONSEQUENCE

HEAVENLY FATHER LET'S ME MAKE MY OWN CHOICES

D&C 58-59

READ D&C 58:1-14

Why do some blessings only come after tribulation?

_____

_____

_____

_____

_____

READ D&C 58:15-30

What are some things in which you are "anxiously engaged"?

_____

_____

_____

_____

_____

READ D&C 58:31-49

How does confessing your sin help you in the repentance process?

_____

_____

_____

_____

_____

READ D&C 59:13-24

How do you keep the Sabbath day holy?

_____

_____

_____

_____

JUNE 9-15

In D&C 60-62, we learn truths about Jesus. Color the picture of Jesus below.

THE SCRIPTURES TEACH OF JESUS

D&C 60-63

MONDAY: READ D&C 60

Do you ever not share your testimony because of "fear of man"? Why?

_____

_____

_____

_____

_____

THURSDAY: READ D&C 62

God doesn't always tell us specifically what to do. Why is this good for us?

_____

_____

_____

_____

_____

READ D&C 63:1-31

What do you do to keep your thoughts chaste?

_____

_____

_____

_____

_____

READ D&C 63:32-66

What sacred things from God should we treat with reverence?

_____

_____

_____

_____

JUNE 16-22

CIRCLE THE DAYS YOU READ THIS WEEK: MON TUES WED THUR FRI SAT SUN

In D&C 64:33-34, we learn that Jesus wants us to follow Him with our hearts and a "willing mind". How can we give our thoughts (minds) and desires (hearts) to the Lord? Fill in the missing words from these scripture verses below.

"WHEREFORE, BE NOT _____ IN _____, FOR YE ARE LAYING THE _____ OF A _____ WORK. AND OUT OF _____ THINGS PROCEEDETH THAT WHICH IS _____.

BEHOLD, THE LORD _____ THE _____ AND A WILLING _____; AND THE WILLING AND _____ SHALL EAT THE _____ OF THE LAND OF _____ IN THESE _____ DAYS."

-D&C 64:33-34

D&C 64-66

READ D&C 64:1-11

Is there someone in your life you need to forgive? Why can forgiveness be difficult?

_____

_____

_____

_____

_____

READ D&C 64:12-34

How can we give our hearts and minds to God?

_____

_____

_____

_____

_____

READ D&C 65

What does the Lord want His kingdom to accomplish on the earth? How can you help?

_____

_____

_____

_____

_____

READ D&C 66:1-7

What do you think God's will is for your life? See verse 4.

_____

_____

_____

_____

_____

JUNE 23-29

In D&C 67, we read that the revelations Joseph Smith had received were published in a book called The Book of Commandments. We have four books of scripture, which we call the Standard Works, that we can read and study to learn about Jesus. Match each book below with the correct description.

THE BIBLE

THE BOOK OF MORMON

THE PEARL OF GREAT PRICE

THE DOCTRINE AND COVENANTS

RECORD OF THE ANCIENT PEOPLE WHO LIVED IN THE AMERICAS THAT TESTIFIES OF CHRIST.

A BOOK CONTAINING LATTER-DAY REVELATIONS & DECLARATIONS.

CONTAINS EXCERPTS FROM JOSEPH SMITH'S TRANSLATION OF GENESIS, MATTHEW 24, TRANSLATION OF SOME EGYPTIAN PAPYRUS (BOOK OF ABRAHAM), AND AN EXCERPT FROM JOSEPH SMITH'S HISTORY

THIS BOOK CONTAINS THE OLD AND NEW TESTAMENT AND IS A COLLECTION OF WRITINGS BY PROPHETS TESTIFYING OF JESUS.

THE SCRIPTURES TEACH ME ABOUT JESUS

D&C 67-70

READ D&C 67
How do we overcome the "natural man" and continue in patience?

_____

_____

_____

_____

_____

_____

READ D&C 68:1-10
What "signs" follow the faithful?

_____

_____

_____

_____

_____

_____

READ D&C 68:25-35
How can you center your home around Jesus Christ?

_____

_____

_____

_____

_____

_____

READ D&C 69
Why is it important to have "true and faithful" friends?

_____

_____

_____

_____

_____

_____

In D&C 72:2, we learn about a person who is called to help us. Crack the code to find out who this person is.

CRACK THE CODE

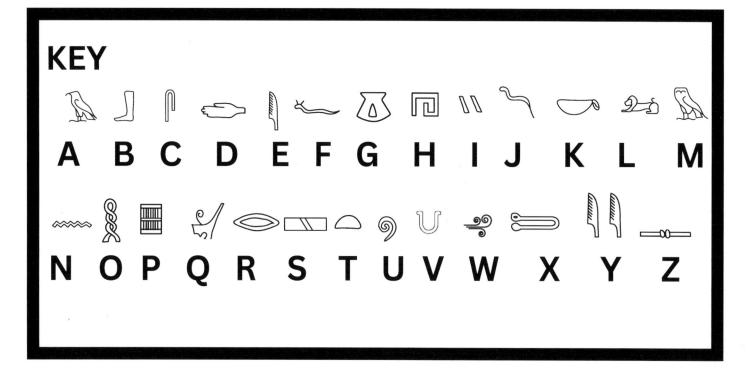

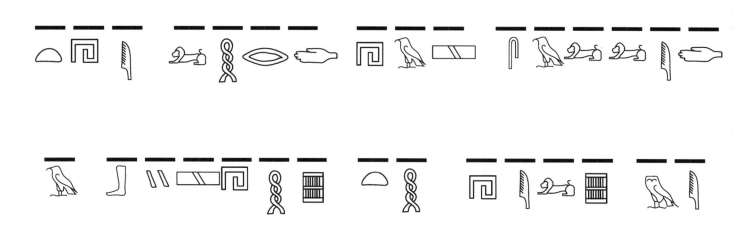

D&C 71-75

READ D&C 71

What can you do to correct falsehoods when someone criticizes your faith?

_____
_____
_____
_____
_____
_____

READ D&C 72

How have you been blessed by the service of a bishop?

_____
_____
_____
_____
_____
_____

READ D&C 75:1-16

What does it mean to be "idle" in sharing the gospel? How are you idle?

_____
_____
_____
_____
_____
_____

READ D&C 75:17-36

Why is the ability to work a blessing in our lives?

_____
_____
_____
_____
_____

JULY 7-13

In D&C 76, we learn about the three degrees of glory and God's Plan of Salvation. Match each degree of glory with the description of the relationship the people had with Christ below.

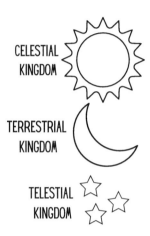

CELESTIAL KINGDOM

TERRESTRIAL KINGDOM

TELESTIAL KINGDOM

THOSE WHO REJECTED CHRIST AND HIS GOSPEL; PEOPLE WHO WERE MURDERERS, LIARS, THIEVES, ADULTERERS

RECEIVED A TESTIMONY OF CHRIST, MADE AND KEPT COVENANTS WITH CHRIST

HONORABLE PEOPLE "WHO WERE BLINDED BY THE CRAFTINESS OF MEN" - REJECTED CHRIST ON EARTH BUT ACCEPTED HIM IN SPIRIT WORLD

In D&C 76:22-24, we learn we are all sons and daughters of God. Complete the scripture verses below with the correct words.

"AND NOW, AFTER THE MANY TESTIMONIES WHICH HAVE BEEN GIVEN OF HIM, THIS IS THE _____, LAST OF ALL, WHICH WE GIVE OF HIM: THAT HE _____! FOR WE SAW _____, EVEN ON THE _____ HAND OF GOD; AND WE HEARD THE _____ BEARING RECORD THAT HE IS THE _____ BEGOTTEN OF THE FATHER—THAT BY HIM, AND THROUGH HIM, AND OF HIM, THE _____ ARE AND WERE CREATED, AND THE INHABITANTS THEREOF ARE BEGOTTEN _____ AND _____ UNTO GOD."
-D&C 76:22-24

HEAVENLY FATHER WANTS ME TO RETURN TO LIVE WITH HIM FOREVER

D&C 76; VOICES OF THE RESTORATION: TESTIMONIES OF "THE VISION"

READ D&C 76:25-49

What do you learn about Satan in these verses?

_____

_____

_____

_____

_____

_____

READ D&C 76:50-70

What kind of relationship do those who inherit Celestial Kingdom have with Christ?

_____

_____

_____

_____

_____

_____

READ D&C 76:71-95

What kind of relationship do those who inherit Terrestrial Kingdom have with Christ?

_____

_____

_____

_____

_____

_____

READ D&C 76:96-119

What kind of relationship do those who inherit Telestial Kingdom have with Christ?

_____

_____

_____

_____

_____

_____

JULY 14-20

In D&C 77:2, we read that God created beasts, creeping things, and fowls of the air. Complete the word search with words related to this verse below.

```
F  Q  X  I  C  C  W  U  B  G  B  B  S  K  K  P  J  K  N  D
Q  U  M  M  M  V  L  T  N  M  Q  G  V  H  M  R  U  O  J  M
G  B  R  E  I  J  Z  I  U  A  N  D  D  C  H  A  S  H  Y  G
V  C  G  T  O  S  P  A  D  I  R  H  K  U  S  E  D  M  F  W
J  Q  Y  R  C  E  Q  S  H  C  P  H  S  M  S  P  E  Y  U  U
A  Q  G  P  E  B  L  T  O  C  V  Z  V  C  G  H  P  M  O  U
O  T  D  R  K  W  J  N  G  N  R  I  E  C  R  U  G  K  V  U
V  J  C  W  O  S  T  S  A  E  B  E  W  N  H  O  J  C  S  D
K  W  V  F  Q  L  E  D  F  K  Z  K  A  X  D  V  H  V  Y  N
N  M  Z  T  S  S  Y  A  N  N  X  W  J  T  M  N  H  G  U  Y
S  C  Z  X  V  O  H  T  T  Y  F  P  B  F  E  E  A  I  Q  W
O  O  R  B  S  W  T  O  G  G  N  U  D  F  A  D  H  T  U  U
O  K  E  Y  U  I  O  M  A  A  S  I  J  V  F  L  P  C  D  A
O  C  C  U  E  V  H  L  I  S  H  A  E  Y  M  X  Y  J  N  S
J  J  D  Q  D  V  W  R  U  W  W  N  K  Q  D  A  P  J  S  O
S  X  G  J  E  U  I  L  I  F  Y  A  X  R  S  E  O  G  A  M
S  Z  R  Z  F  V  J  D  E  L  K  I  A  U  U  L  O  L  I  U
Z  L  X  E  R  C  G  E  J  H  P  J  H  J  Z  X  X  I  X  Z
N  X  M  K  J  U  C  H  R  P  D  O  D  E  X  K  W  Z  M  U
K  E  N  Y  N  J  H  X  U  K  Y  N  T  W  T  I  U  R  G  I
```

JOHN	GOD	CREATED
BEASTS	CREEPING	THINGS
FOWLS	AIR	HEAVEN

GOD CREATED EVERY CREATURE ON EARTH

D&C 77-80

READ REVELATION CHAPTERS 4-11

What questions do you have after reading these chapters?

_____

_____

_____

_____

_____

_____

READ D&C 77

Did this section answer your questions listed above? What did you learn?

_____

_____

_____

_____

_____

_____

READ D&C 78:11-22

How does being grateful bless your life?

_____

_____

_____

_____

_____

_____

READ D&C 79 & 80

Why is serving the Lord more important than where you serve?

_____

_____

_____

_____

_____

JULY 21-27

READ D&C 81

Has reading this section made you think of someone you could "lift up" this week?

_____
_____
_____
_____
_____
_____

READ D&C 82:7-12

How is the Lord "bound" when we follow His commandments?

_____
_____
_____
_____
_____
_____

READ D&C 82:19-24

How can you seek "interest" of your neighbor?

_____
_____
_____
_____
_____
_____

READ D&C 83

How can you help widows, single-parents, orphans, or others in need?

_____
_____
_____
_____
_____

D&C 81-83

In D&C 81:5, we read that we should help those in need. Jesus was the perfect example of helping the weak. With your family or individually, think of examples from the scriptures of Jesus helping others. In the top row, write what the picture could be showing. In the bottom squares, draw or write your own examples of ways Jesus helped others.

JESUS HELPED THOSE IN NEED & I CAN, TOO

JULY 28-AUGUST 3

In D&C 84:19-22, we learn about the importance of priesthood ordinances. Fill in the missing words from D&C 84:20-22 below.

"THEREFORE, IN THE _____ THEREOF, THE _____ OF GODLINESS IS MANIFEST. AND WITHOUT THE ORDINANCES THEREOF, AND THE _____ OF THE _____, THE POWER OF _____ IS NOT MANIFEST UNTO MEN IN THE _____; FOR WITHOUT THIS NO _____ CAN SEE THE FACE OF _____, EVEN THE FATHER, AND _____"
-D&C 84:20-22

Unscramble the words below that are priesthood ordinances. Other ordinances not listed below include ordaining to priesthood offices, consecrating oil, administering to the sick, anointing with oil, sealing the anointing, father's blessings, blessings of comfort and guidance, dedicating graves.

SBPTIMA _____

ACSAMETRN _____

ONIRMTCIONFA _____

I CAN RECEIVE HEAVENLY FATHER'S POWER THROUGH PRIESTHOOD ORDINANCES

D&C 84

MONDAY: READ D&C 84:1-20

What do you learn about the New Jerusalem in these verses?

_____
_____
_____
_____
_____

TUESDAY: READ D&C 84:21-40

What would your life look like without priesthood ordinances?

_____
_____
_____
_____
_____

WEDNESDAY: READ D&C 84:41-60

Why do we need to consistently study the word of God?

_____
_____
_____
_____
_____

FRIDAY: READ D&C 84:81-100

How does the Lord support you in the work He has asked you to do in your life?

_____
_____
_____
_____
_____

AUGUST 4-10

CIRCLE THE DAYS YOU READ THIS WEEK: MON TUES WED THUR FRI SAT SUN

In D&C 86, we learn more about the parable of the wheat and the tares from Matthew 13. We can help gather the "wheat" (God's people). Match the pictures to the correct definition below as you read D&C 86.

WHEAT

THOSE WHO FOLLOW SATAN

TARES

CHRIST AND HIS APOSTLES

FIELD

THE RIGHTEOUS

SOWER OF SEEDS

THE WORLD

THE ENEMY

END OF THE WORLD

THE HARVEST

THE DEVIL & HIS POWER

I CAN GATHER GOD'S PEOPLE

D&C 85-87

READ D&C 85:1-6

What could you record about your life that could be a blessing to future generations?

_____

_____

_____

_____

_____

READ D&C 85:7-12

How does the spirit speak to you?

_____

_____

_____

_____

_____

READ D&C 87:1-4

What do you learn about prophesy from this revelation?

_____

_____

_____

_____

_____

READ D&C 87:5-8

What are some "holy places" in your life?

_____

_____

_____

_____

_____

AUGUST 11-17

In D&C 88:77-80, 118, we learn that it is important to the Lord that we learn. Write or draw answers to the questions below.

WHY HE WANTS ME TO LEARN
D&C 88:80

WHAT THE LORD WANTS ME TO LEARN
D&C 88:77-79

HOW WE SHOULD LEARN
D&C 88:118

HEAVENLY FATHER WANTS ME TO LEARN

D&C 88

READ D&C 88:24-48

How do we obey the laws of the degrees of glory in this life?

_____

_____

_____

_____

_____

_____

READ D&C 88:49-73

How do you "draw near" unto Christ in your life?

_____

_____

_____

_____

_____

_____

READ D&C 88:74-98

Why is education important to the Lord?

_____

_____

_____

_____

_____

READ D&C 88:99-122

How can we make our home like the temple?

_____

_____

_____

_____

_____

_____

AUGUST 18-24

In D&C 89, the Lord gives us a Word of Wisdom to keep our bodies and spirits healthy. A good way to avoid temptation is to make a plan now on how you would respond when you are offered something that is against the Word of Wisdom. Answer the questions below.

HOW WOULD YOU RESPOND TO A FRIEND THAT OFFERS A "SIP" OF BEER OR ALCOHOL?

HOW WOULD YOU RESPOND TO A FRIEND THAT PRESSURES YOU TO TRY VAPING?

A FRIEND OFFERS YOU AN ICED COFFEE. WHAT DO YOU SAY?

THE WORD OF WISDOM KEEPS MY BODY & SPIRIT HEALTHY

To read more info on parts of the Word of Wisdom youth may be confused about, visit https://www.churchofjesuschrist.org/study/new-era/2019/08/vaping-coffee-tea-and-marijuana

D&C 89-92

READ D&C 89:1-11

Have you seen "evils and designs … in the hearts of conspiring men" in regards to the Word of Wisdom?

_____

_____

_____

_____

READ D&C 89:12-21

Are there any specific ways you are prompted to take better care of your body?

_____

_____

_____

_____

_____

READ D&C 90:26-37

What warnings does the Lord give in these verses?

_____

_____

_____

_____

_____

READ D&C 91 & 92

How has the spirit helped you discern truth in your life?

_____

_____

_____

_____

_____

AUGUST 25-31

In D&C 93:2-21, we learn many important truths about the Savior. One of those truths is listed below, but you must crack the code to figure out what it is.

CRACK THE CODE

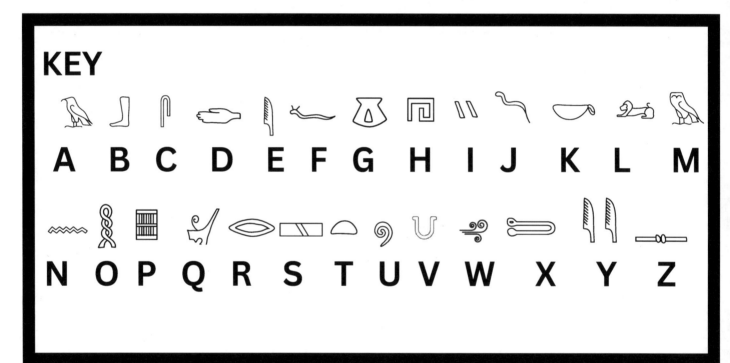

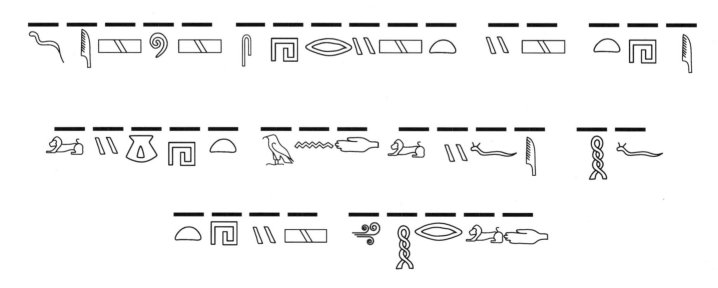

D&C 93

READ D&C 93:1-9

How is Jesus the light of the world?

_____
_____
_____
_____
_____
_____

READ D&C 93:10-20

What does it mean to receive "grace for grace"?

_____
_____
_____
_____
_____
_____

READ D&C 93:31-40

What do you learn about light and truth in these verses?

_____
_____
_____
_____
_____
_____

READ D&C 93:41-53

How are you setting your house in order?

_____
_____
_____
_____
_____
_____

SEPTEMBER 1-7

READ D&C 94
What stands out to you about the Lord's directions for these buildings?

_____
_____
_____
_____
_____

READ D&C 95:1-8
What do we learn in this section about how to give correction to others?

_____
_____
_____
_____
_____

READ D&C 95:9-17
What does the temple mean to you?

_____
_____
_____
_____
_____

READ D&C 96
What can you do to help strengthen your stake?

_____
_____
_____
_____
_____

D&C 94-97

In D&C 95:8, we read why the Lord wants us to build temples. The Kirtland Temple was the first temple in this dispensation. What other reasons do we build temples?

WHY WE BUILD TEMPLES:

_____

_____

_____

_____

_____

_____

_____

_____

_____

_____

HOUSE OF THE LORD

THE TEMPLE IS THE HOUSE OF THE LORD

SEPTEMBER 8-14

In D&C 98:1-24, we learn about trials the Saints in Missouri were experiencing. In 1833, the Saints were driven out through violence. What trials do you have in your life? Have any of your trials ever turned to a blessing?

SAINTS IN MISSOURI WERE NOT TREATED KINDLY BY OTHERS AND EVENTUALLY HAD TO LEAVE THEIR HOMES

TRIALS I'VE HAD IN MY LIFE:

_____

_____

_____

_____

_____

_____

TRIALS THAT TURNED INTO A BLESSING IN MY LIFE:

_____

_____

_____

_____

_____

_____

JESUS CAN TURN MY TRIALS INTO BLESSINGS

D&C 98-101

READ D&C 98:25-48

Do you see any advice in these verses that could help you handle personal conflicts?

_____

_____

_____

_____

_____

READ D&C 100

Do you think the Lord would refer to you as His friend? Why or why not? (see vs. 1)

_____

_____

_____

_____

_____

_____

READ D&C 101:1-50

What will life be like when Jesus comes again?

_____

_____

_____

_____

_____

READ D&C 101:51-101

What do you learn from the parable of the nobleman and the olive trees?

_____

_____

_____

_____

_____

SEPTEMBER 15-21

READ D&C 102
What is the purpose of councils in the Church?

_____
_____
_____
_____
_____

READ D&C 103
Why did the Lord allow the Saints to lose their land in Missouri?

_____
_____
_____
_____
_____

READ D&C 104:1-41
What do we learn about handling our finances in these verses?

_____
_____
_____
_____
_____

READ D&C 104:42-86
How have you been blessed by following the commandments? (see vs. 42)

_____
_____
_____
_____
_____

D&C 102-105; VOICES OF THE RESTORATION: ZION'S CAMP

READ D&C 105

What principles is Zion to be built upon?

_____

_____

_____

_____

_____

_____

READ VOICES OF THE RESTORATION: ZION'S CAMP

What do you learn about Zion's camp from this reading?

_____

_____

_____

_____

_____

_____

_____

WAYS I CAN BE A LIGHT TO THE WORLD:

_____

_____

_____

_____

_____

_____

_____

D&C 103:9

SEPTEMBER 22-28

CIRCLE THE DAYS YOU READ THIS WEEK: MON TUES WED THUR FRI SAT SUN

READ D&C 107:1-25

How do we uphold the Lord's servants through our faith, prayers, and confidence?

_____

_____

_____

_____

_____

READ D&C 107:26-50

How has your testimony been strengthened by the apostles?

_____

_____

_____

_____

_____

READ D&C 107:76-100

What is the responsibility of all who accept a call to the priesthood? (see vs. 99-100)

_____

_____

_____

_____

_____

READ D&C 108

What vows have you made with God? Are you "careful" in keeping them?

_____

_____

_____

_____

_____

D&C 106-108

In D&C 108:3, we read that we should be careful in observing our covenants. In the examples below, draw a line to either "careful" or "casual" to decide how the person is behaving in that situation.

 LUKE READS THE COME, FOLLOW ME LESSON EACH WEEK & IS PREPARED TO PARTICIPATE IN CLASS & GIVE INSIGHTFUL COMMENTS.

SOFIE WATCHES A TV SHOW HER FRIENDS AT SCHOOL ALWAYS ARE TALKING ABOUT, EVEN THOUGH IT USES INAPPROPRIATE LANGUAGE AND HAS QUESTIONABLE CONTENT.

CAREFUL *or* CASUAL

 GREY PLAYS GAMES ON HIS PHONE WHILE THE SACRAMENT IS BEING PASSED.

 OLIVIA GETS INTO BED & THEN REMEMBERS SHE FORGOT TO SAY HER PRAYERS. SHE DECIDES SHE WILL JUST DO IT TOMORROW AS SHE IS TOO COMFORTABLE TO KNEEL.

I CAN BE CAREFUL IN LIVING MY COVENANTS

SEPTEMBER 29-OCTOBER 5

CIRCLE THE DAYS YOU READ THIS WEEK: MON TUES WED THUR FRI SAT SUN

READ D&C 109:1-20

How do you feel the Lord's power in the temple?

_____

_____

_____

_____

_____

READ D&C 109:21-40

How does the Lord help His work to continue, despite persecution?

_____

_____

_____

_____

_____

READ D&C 109:41-60

How do we see things in this dedicatory prayer being fulfilled today?

_____

_____

_____

_____

_____

READ VOICES OF THE RESTORATION: SPIRITUAL MANIFESTATIONS & THE KIRTLAND TEMPLE

Write down any feelings and thoughts from this reading.

_____

_____

_____

_____

_____

D&C 109-110; VOICES OF THE RESTORATION: SPIRITUAL MANIFESTATIONS & THE KIRTLAND TEMPLE

In D&C 110, we learn of heavenly beings who visited Joseph Smith and Oliver Cowdery in the Kirtland temple and restored priesthood keys. Match the heavenly beings with the priesthood keys they restored.

ELIAS

ELIJAH

MOSES

THE SAVIOR BLESSES US THROUGH PRIESTHOOD KEYS

OCTOBER 6-12

CIRCLE THE DAYS YOU READ THIS WEEK: MON TUES WED THUR FRI SAT SUN

READ D&C 111

How does the Lord help you when you are worried about something?

_____
_____
_____
_____
_____

READ D&C 112:11-21

How can we continually nourish our testimonies to be converted to Jesus Christ?

_____
_____
_____
_____
_____

READ D&C 112:22-34

What darkness do you see on the earth today?

_____
_____
_____
_____
_____

READ D&C 113

What do we learn about the role of Joseph Smith from Isaiah?

_____
_____
_____

D&C 111-114

In D&C 112:10, we learn that if we are humble the Lord will lead us and give us answers to our prayers. In D&C 112:11, we learn that we should love everyone. Complete the word search below with words from these verses.

```
K  L  P  Y  L  O  V  E  V  N  B  A  T  C  A
B  E  L  J  T  B  K  L  L  P  T  S  K  M  R
T  A  L  K  J  N  M  H  X  X  R  G  S  G  W
Q  D  K  V  Y  M  E  X  M  E  F  V  Q  I  D
G  H  H  B  I  F  P  P  W  S  V  F  U  Z  T
W  M  Z  R  L  V  T  S  R  K  M  V  P  F  X
V  T  Z  N  E  E  N  T  O  A  C  T  S  Q  Z
M  V  Q  W  L  A  S  T  M  A  Y  A  C  H  D
V  M  R  B  F  G  J  S  I  C  L  E  I  O  M
R  A  M  H  J  H  O  P  I  K  R  Q  R  Y  V
Y  U  Y  B  W  W  G  O  F  N  I  P  Q  S  T
H  P  J  Z  O  Z  Y  J  A  T  G  G  G  L  G
F  J  C  L  X  V  E  A  W  S  G  S  D  U  I
U  H  X  H  A  N  D  T  R  U  S  T  J  E  V
E  V  E  R  Y  O  N  E  F  U  V  C  W  E  E
```

HUMBLE	LEAD	HAND
GIVE	ANSWERS	PRAYER
BLESSINGS	LOVE	EVERYONE

THE LORD WILL LEAD ME BY THE HAND & ANSWER MY PRAYERS

OCTOBER 13-19

READ D&C 115:1-9
What spiritual storms do you notice around you?

_____
_____
_____
_____
_____
_____

READ D&C 115:4-5
What is the significance of the name of the Lord's Church?

_____
_____
_____
_____
_____
_____

READ D&C 116 & 117
What sacrifices do you make for God in your life?

_____
_____
_____
_____
_____
_____

READ D&C 118
Why do you think some of the early apostles of the church apostatized?

_____
_____
_____
_____
_____
_____

In D&C 119, the Lord gives the Law of Tithing. We are to give one-tenth of our earnings to the Lord. In the circles below write some ways your tithing is used. Ask your family for ideas, if needed.

HEAVENLY FATHER USES TITHING TO BLESS HIS CHILDREN

OCTOBER 20-26

CIRCLE THE DAYS YOU READ THIS WEEK: MON TUES WED THUR FRI SAT SUN

READ D&C 121:16-30

Why must we be judged of our works?

_____

_____

_____

_____

_____

READ D&C 121:31-46

What does it mean that "many are called but few are chosen"?

_____

_____

_____

_____

_____

READ D&C 123

How can we cheerfully go about doing the Lord's work despite wickedness in the world?

_____

_____

_____

_____

_____

READ VOICES OF THE RESTORATION: LIBERTY JAIL

Write any impressions from these passages written by Emma and Joseph.

_____

_____

_____

_____

_____

D&C 121-123;
VOICES OF THE RESTORATION: LIBERTY JAIL

In D&C 123:15-17, we learn that small things can make a big difference. Like a small helm of a ship steers the large vessel, our small efforts can also make a big difference. Think of small ways you can serve your family and friends this week and write the ways in the circles below.

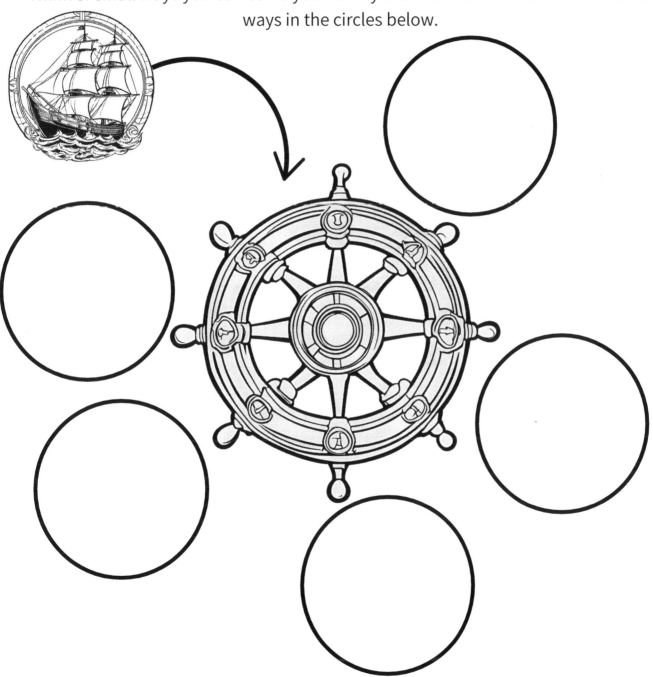

SMALL EFFORTS CAN MAKE A BIG DIFFERENCE

OCTOBER 27-NOVEMBER 2

CIRCLE THE DAYS YOU READ THIS WEEK: MON TUES WED THUR FRI SAT SUN

After facing much persecution in both Kirtland and Missouri, the Saints in Ohio and Missouri left in 1838 and gathered in Illinois. There they built the city of Nauvoo on swampy land next to the Mississippi River. In D&C 124:28-29, 39, the Lord commands the Saints to build a temple in Nauvoo. Draw your own sunstone in the blank column below, using the example for guidance.

FINISH DRAWING THE SUNSTONE FOR THE NAUVOO TEMPLE

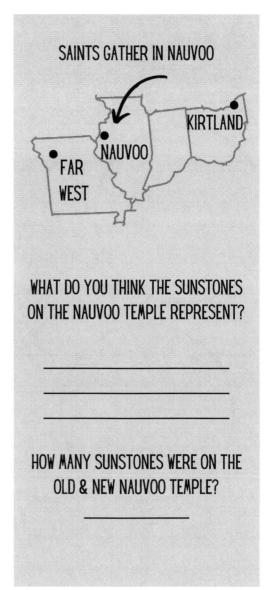

SAINTS GATHER IN NAUVOO

WHAT DO YOU THINK THE SUNSTONES ON THE NAUVOO TEMPLE REPRESENT?

_____
_____
_____

HOW MANY SUNSTONES WERE ON THE OLD & NEW NAUVOO TEMPLE?

_____

JESUS CHRIST COMMANDS HIS PEOPLE TO BUILD TEMPLES

Answer: Sun represents the Restoration & the Gospel bringing light to the Earth; 30 sunstones on both the old and new Nauvoo temples

D&C 124; VOICES OF THE RESTORATION: THE RELIEF SOCIETY

READ D&C 124:1-29

What do we learn in these verses about complimenting others on their Godly attributes?

_____

_____

_____

_____

_____

READ D&C 124:90-119

How is your patriarchal blessing a guide in your life? If you don't have one, how can you prepare to receive yours?

_____

_____

_____

_____

_____

READ D&C 124:120-145

How can we magnify our callings when asked to serve?

_____

_____

_____

_____

_____

READ VOICES OF THE RESTORATION: THE RELIEF SOCIETY

What did you learn from this reading?

_____

_____

_____

_____

_____

NOVEMBER 3-9

CIRCLE THE DAYS YOU READ THIS WEEK: MON TUES WED THUR FRI SAT SUN

READ D&C 125

How does asking God a question open the door to receive revelation?

_____

_____

_____

_____

_____

READ D&C 126

What can you do to care for your family?

_____

_____

_____

_____

_____

READ D&C 127

How does the Lord help you through "deep water" in your life?

_____

_____

_____

_____

_____

READ VOICES OF THE RESTORATION: BAPTISM FOR OUR ANCESTORS

What did you learn about baptisms for the dead in this reading?

_____

_____

_____

_____

D&C 125-128; VOICES OF THE RESTORATION: BAPTISM FOR OUR ANCESTORS, "A GLORIOUS DOCTRINE"

In D&C 128:5, 12, we learn that all God's children will have the opportunity to be baptized. In the temple, we can baptize those who have died without the ordinance through a proxy baptism. Complete the cross-word puzzle below with words related to this topic.

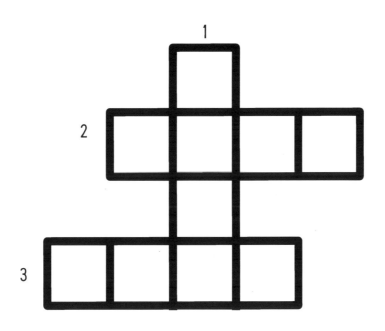

DOWN

1-OUR ANCESTORS WHO WERE NOT BAPTIZED IN THIS _____ NEED US TO DO THEIR ORDINANCES ON THEIR BEHALF.

ACROSS

2-BAPTISMS IN THE TEMPLE ARE PERFORMED FOR THOSE WHO HAVE _____ WITHOUT KNOWLEDGE OF THE GOSPEL.

3-THE TEMPLE BAPTISMAL FONT IS RESTING ON 12 _____

ALL GOD'S CHILDREN SHOULD HAVE OPPORTUNITY TO BE BAPTIZED

NOVEMBER 10-16

In D&C 130:22, we learn that Heavenly Father and Jesus Christ have a physical body, but the Holy Ghost does not. Fill in the missing words from this scripture verse.

"THE _____ HAS A _____ OF FLESH AND _____ AS TANGIBLE AS MAN'S; THE _____ ALSO; BUT THE HOLY _____ HAS NOT A BODY OF _____ AND BONES, BUT IS A PERSONAGE OF _____ WERE IT NOT SO, THE HOLY GHOST COULD NOT _____ IN US."
-D&C 130:22

SON GHOST FATHER FLESH BODY SPIRIT BONES DWELL

Draw a picture of Jesus and Heavenly Father below.

HEAVENLY FATHER & JESUS HAVE AN IMMORTAL PHYSICAL BODY

D&C 129-132

READ D&C 129

What did you learn about angels in this section?

_____

_____

_____

_____

_____

READ D&C 130

What impressions about obedience did you have after reading this section?

_____

_____

_____

_____

_____

READ D&C 131

What did you learn about the importance of being married and sealed in the temple?

_____

_____

_____

_____

READ D&C 132:46-66

What counsel was Emma Smith given? How can that apply to you?

_____

_____

_____

_____

_____

NOVEMBER 17-23

READ D&C 133:1-15

What are you doing to leave "Babylon" and go to "Zion"?

_____

_____

_____

_____

_____

_____

READ D&C 133:57-74

Why is the Gospel being sent forth to all the world?

_____

_____

_____

_____

_____

_____

READ D&C 134

What are the principles of government? What are your responsibilities as a citizen?

_____

_____

_____

_____

_____

READ "THE FUTURE OF THE CHURCH: PREPARING THE WORLD FOR THE SAVIOR'S SECOND COMING" BY PRES. NELSON, LIAHONA, APR. 2020

What stood out to you in this talk?

_____

_____

_____

_____

D&C 133-134

In D&C 134:1-2, we read the Lord wants us to obey the law. What would life be like if we didn't have any rules and laws? Match the laws broken with the potential consequences if we didn't have these laws or no one obeyed them.

 NOT STOPPING AT A RED LIGHT

COULD HIT A CHILD & INJURE OR KILL THEM

 NOT PAYING FOR ITEMS AT THE STORE

CITIES WOULD BE DANGEROUS IF THERE WERE NO CONSEQUENCE FOR HURTING OTHERS

 SPEEDING THROUGH A SCHOOL ZONE

YOU COULD HIT ANOTHER CAR GOING THROUGH THE INTERSECTION

 BEATING SOMEONE UP

STORES WOULD GO OUT OF BUSINESS IF NO ONE PAID FOR ITEMS

 DRIVING THE WRONG WAY ON A ONE-WAY STREET

COULD HIT ANOTHER VEHICLE HEAD-ON AND CAUSE INJURIES OR DEATH

THE LORD WANTS ME TO OBEY THE LAW

NOVEMBER 24-30

In D&C 135:3, we read of the many great things Joseph Smith did during his life. He and his brother, Hyrum, were murdered in Carthage Jail. On the hearts below, write some of the things Joseph did during his life that have changed your life.

JOSEPH SMITH WAS A PROPHET

D&C 135-136

READ D&C 136:1-10

How was the Camp of Israel to be organized?

_____

_____

_____

_____

_____

READ D&C 136:11-20

What counsel is given to the Saints?

_____

_____

_____

_____

_____

READ D&C 136:21-30

How was the Saints conduct in their journey west just as important as reaching their destination?

_____

_____

_____

_____

_____

READ D&C 136:31-42

Why are prophets killed?

_____

_____

_____

_____

_____

DECEMBER 1-7

In D&C 138:1-11, we read about what helps us better understand the scriptures. Crack the code to see what we should do.

CRACK THE CODE

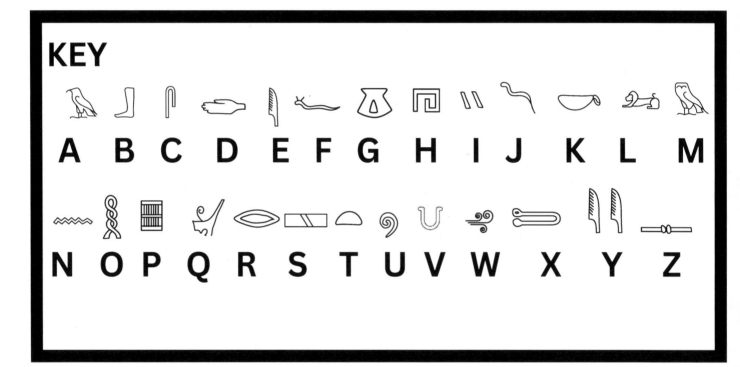

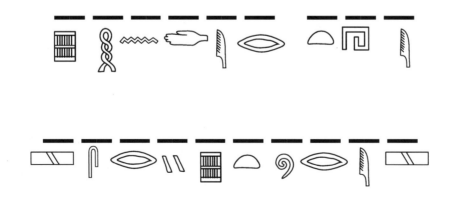

D&C 137-138

READ D&C 137

What do you know because of this revelation?

_____

_____

_____

_____

_____

READ D&C 138:1-15

What changes does this section inspire you to make to receive more personal revelation?

_____

_____

_____

_____

_____

READ D&C 138:16-30

What did President Smith see in these verses?

_____

_____

_____

_____

_____

READ D&C 138:31-45

Why is it important for us to know the work that is happening in the spirit world?

_____

_____

_____

_____

_____

DECEMBER 8-14

The Articles of Faith explain what The Church of Jesus Christ of Latter-day Saints believes. Write the correct Article of Faith number with it's corresponding summary in the hearts below.

#__ GATHERING OF ISRAEL

#__ ATONEMENT

#__ GODHEAD

#__ PRINCIPLES OF GOSPEL

#__ BEING HONEST

#__ PUNISHED FOR OWN TRANSGRESSIONS

#__ OBEYING LAW

#__ CALLED OF GOD BY...

#__ SAME ORGANIZATION AS PRIMITIVE CHURCH

#__ GIFTS

#__ WORD OF GOD

#__ ALL GOD REVEALS

#__ WORSHIP GOD

I BELIEVE IN JESUS' GOSPEL

THE ARTICLES OF FAITH & OFFICIAL DECLARATIONS 1&2

READ THE ARTICLES OF FAITH

How can you use the Articles of Faith to share the Gospel with others?

_____
_____
_____
_____
_____
_____

READ THE ARTICLES OF FAITH

Do you have a favorite Article of Faith? Which one and why?

_____
_____
_____
_____
_____
_____

READ OFFICIAL DECLARATION 1

Why did the Lord end the practice of plural marriage among the Saints?

_____
_____
_____
_____
_____
_____

READ OFFICIAL DECLARATION 2

How have you learned to trust the Lord even when you don't have perfect understanding?

_____
_____
_____
_____
_____

DECEMBER 15-21

READ PARAGRAPH 3 OF "THE FAMILY: A PROCLAMATION TO THE WORLD"

How does having a knowledge of the premortal world help guide you here on earth?

_____

_____

_____

_____

_____

_____

READ PARAGRAPHS 6&7 OF "THE FAMILY: A PROCLAMATION TO THE WORLD"

Can you think of a family relationship you would like to strengthen? How will you do that?

_____

_____

_____

_____

_____

_____

READ PARAGRAPH 8 OF "THE FAMILY: A PROCLAMATION TO THE WORLD"

Why are families important to society? What happens when they disintegrate?

_____

_____

_____

_____

_____

READ THE LAST PARAGRAPH OF "THE FAMILY: A PROCLAMATION TO THE WORLD"

What is the call to action? What can you do to share the message of this proclamation?

_____

_____

_____

_____

_____

THE FAMILY: A PROCLAMATION TO THE WORLD

In The Family Proclamation, we learn that successful families are built upon certain principles. These principles can be found in the word search below.

```
O  A  C  N  D  K  W  O  J  Q  U  O  F  Q  U
H  T  I  A  F  O  B  Z  M  S  F  O  D  P  U
Q  K  N  T  R  X  S  Q  L  U  R  L  A  H  H
I  J  B  K  L  S  M  D  S  G  Q  Q  R  U  R
S  U  N  O  M  P  O  Q  I  X  J  R  A  N  D
V  H  V  N  S  Z  R  V  V  F  F  U  A  M  L
F  E  V  M  P  I  E  P  S  Y  S  X  K  R  X
A  K  W  Q  P  N  Y  O  N  B  C  S  A  I  B
L  U  S  L  E  I  A  E  R  Y  E  L  W  A  L
F  B  Y  S  A  W  R  G  P  E  T  E  R  Z  V
J  H  S  A  D  M  P  N  U  F  S  A  L  W  M
Z  F  T  E  G  N  O  I  S  S  A  P  M  O  C
D  F  N  O  I  T  A  E  R  C  E  R  E  S  C
K  O  E  R  L  G  K  H  S  P  O  B  N  C  C
S  I  E  C  N  A  T  N  E  P  E  R  F  X  T
```

FAITH	PRAYER	REPENTANCE
FORGIVENESS	RESPECT	LOVE
COMPASSION	WORK	RECREATION

FAMILIES ARE HAPPIEST WHEN THEY FOLLOW JESUS

DECEMBER 22-28

In the second paragraph of the "Living Christ," we see some of the many good things Jesus went about doing. How can you serve others like He did? Color the picture below.

WAYS JESUS SERVED OTHERS:

_____

_____

_____

_____

_____

_____

WAYS I CAN SERVE OTHERS:

_____

_____

_____

_____

_____

_____

JESUS WENT ABOUT DOING GOOD

CHRISTMAS

READ THE LIVING CHRIST: THE TESTIMONY OF THE APOSTLES
Why is the birth of the Savior so important and why do we celebrate it?

_____

_____

_____

_____

_____

READ MATTHEW 1:18-25 & MATTHEW CHAPTER 2
Why was King Herod "troubled" when he heard of the birth of Christ?

_____

_____

_____

_____

_____

READ ROMANS 8:24-25; ETHER 12:4; MORONI 7:41
How does Jesus Christ give you hope?

_____

_____

_____

_____

_____

READ "FOUR GIFTS THAT JESUS CHRIST OFFERS TO YOU" BY PRES. NELSON, FIRST PRESIDENCY CHRISTMAS DEVOTIONAL, DEC. 2, 2018, GOSPEL LIBRARY
What are the four gifts that Jesus has given you?

_____

_____

_____

GOAL REFLECTION

How did you do with your spiritual, physical, social, and intellectual goals this past year? Write about each goal below.

_____
_____
_____
_____
_____
_____
_____
_____
_____
_____
_____
_____
_____

In space below, write your testimony and what you have learned from studying the Doctrine and Covenants this year.

_____
_____
_____
_____
_____
_____
_____
_____
_____
_____
_____
_____
_____
_____

IF YOU ENJOYED THIS BOOK, MAKE SURE TO LEAVE A REVIEW.

CHECK OUT OUR OTHER BOOKS.

FOLLOW US ONLINE!

@LATTER.DAY.DESIGNS

LATTER-DAY DESIGNS

Made in the USA
Coppell, TX
07 January 2025